HAPPY DAYS

James Knowlson is the author of the authorised biography of
Samuel Beckett (*Damned to Fame*, Bloomsbury, 1996).
Founder of the Beckett Archive at Reading and of the Beckett
International Foundation, he is General Editor of *The
Theatrical Notebooks of Samuel Beckett* (Faber, 1992–1999) and
editor of volume IV (*Krapp's Last Tape*) and (with Dougald
McMillan) volume I (*Waiting for Godot*). He is also editor of a
bilingual edition of *Happy Days/Oh les beaux jours* (Faber,
1978) and (with Elizabeth Knowlson) *Beckett Remembering,
Remembering Beckett* (Bloomsbury, 2006).

SAMUEL BECKETT

Happy Days
A play in two acts

Preface by James Knowlson

ff

faber and faber

Originally published in the United States in 1961 by Grove Press
First published in Great Britain by Faber and Faber in 1962

This edition first published in 2010
by Faber and Faber Ltd
Bloomsbury House
74–77 Great Russell Street
London WC1B 3DA

Typeset by RefineCatch Limited, Bungay, Suffolk
Printed in England by CPI Bookmarque, Croydon

All applications for performing should be addressed to:
Curtis Brown Ltd, 4th Floor, Haymarket House,
28/29 Haymarket, London SW1 4SP

A CIP record for this book
is available from the British Library

ISBN 978-0-571-24457-7

2 4 6 8 10 9 7 5 3 1

Contents

Preface

Samuel Beckett wrote his first three full-length plays (*Eleutheria*, *En attendant Godot* and *Fin de partie*) in French. Then, in 1956, after translating some of his recent French prose fiction and *En attendant Godot* and *Fin de partie* into English, he started to write again for the theatre. This time, however, he wrote directly in English. First were two radio plays for the BBC, *All that Fall* and *Embers*, followed by a stage monologue, *Krapp's Last Tape*, written with the distinctively cracked voice of the Northern Ireland actor Patrick Magee resonating in his mind. All three of these plays represented for Beckett a return to his childhood or his youth in Ireland. The action in *All that Fall* centres on the railway station near Beckett's home in Foxrock on the Dublin and South Eastern railway line, near to Leopardstown racecourse. And *Embers* and *Krapp's Last Tape* evoke the coastline and hills of County Dublin, where, in the 1920s and early 1930s, Beckett used to walk for hours on end with his father and their Kerry Blue terrier.

Manuscript drafts of his next play, *Happy Days*, written in English during the autumn and winter months of 1960 and 1961, also show early signs of an Irish setting and background. The song on the musical box which Winnie listens to (and sings movingly at the end of the play) was originally going to be 'When Irish Eyes Are Smiling', before it became the 'Waltz Duet' from Franz Lehár's operetta *The Merry Widow*. Several half-hidden echoes of Irish poems and songs remain deeply embedded in the published text. Just as Winnie's words 'I call to the eye of the mind' quote directly from W. B. Yeats's play *At the Hawk's Well*, so her 'young and foolish' evokes Yeats's poem 'Down by the Salley Gardens' – of which Beckett heard a musical setting only two years before writing *Happy Days*, sung by an American student at a master-class of Marya Freund in Paris. The notion of Winnie smiling in the 'wilderness', as well as her memory of 'a last bumper' of champagne, also probably owes a debt to Thomas Moore's poem 'One Bumper at Parting' in the *Irish Melodies*, which contains the lines 'Those few sunny spots, like the present, that mid the dull wilderness smile', which seem so appropriate to Winnie's situation. But if Winnie's words retain a distinctively Irish inspiration and 'feel', in the finished text she is exiled to the English Home Counties, with memories surfacing of a scene in her adolescence with 'Charlie Hunter' in the garden at Borough Green (or, in an earlier manuscript, 'Sevenoaks') in Kent.

Rewriting the play, Beckett removed most of the localised references (one of which cited an 'aberrant rocket' striking Erin). From the very beginning Winnie had been placed in a strange, barren, hostile, almost Dantesque world, creating, as Ruby Cohn put it, 'a new stage metaphor for the old human condition – burial in a dying earth, exposure under a ruthless sun'.[1] There were many different sources of inspiration for this play, ranging from the literary (Dante's *Divine Comedy*, Milton's *Paradise Lost*, Defoe's *Robinson Crusoe*, among others) to Beckett's own philosophical and psychological readings in the 1930s, as well as to his personal experience of psychoanalysis with W. R. Bion in 1934–5. But Beckett also created a woman whose routine response to the cruel realities of her situation lies in optimistic clichés and ritualised habits. She has, Beckett once said, 'a profound frivolity. She's scatterbrained, she babbles.'[2] In this respect, as well as in her optimism, there may have been a real-life model or models at whose identity we can now only guess.

In the theatre of the early 1960s, before the premise of *Happy Days* became familiar, the starkness and boldness of the play's opening tableau provoked immediate surprise or even bewilderment in spectators, confronted as they were with the startling presence of a woman buried up to her waist in the ground, yet who behaves as if this were the most natural thing in the world. No explanation is offered in the play for Winnie's progressive entombment in the earth or for the isolated situation in which she and her husband, Willie, find themselves, surviving like two castaways on or in a mound of scorched grass, in a deserted landscape, away from all other human beings. This opening image can still surprise or shock us today, fifty years on. Simplicity and barrenness of setting have always been primary characteristics of the Beckettian stage world. In *En attendant Godot* (*Waiting for Godot*), there is only a single tree – leafless in the first act – on a country road. In *Fin de partie* (*Endgame*), the bleak set consists of an ill-lit room almost without furniture, with two windows looking out on what appears to be a dead, or dying, world. The acting area in *Krapp's Last Tape* (*La Dernière bande*) is bare: save for a single table and chair placed in a zone of bright light, the rest of the stage is shrouded in darkness. The sets of Beckett's later short plays – *Play, Come and Go, That Time, Footfalls, A Piece of Monologue, Rockaby, Ohio Impromptu* – have been no less stark and austere.

In *Happy Days*, however, the world inhabited by Winnie and her partner, Willie, is extreme and elemental as well as simple and barren. The division of light and darkness which nuances so many of Beckett's plays has disappeared, leaving only the searing light of the sun. Traditionally, of course, light has been regarded as an essential attribute of Heaven, and, throughout the play, Winnie makes a desperate attempt to convert her barren world, a most unpromising Eden, into a joy-filled, sunlit paradise, greeting her new 'day' with a tribute to the light ('another heavenly day') and responding to the most laconic pronouncement from Willie as a source (or promise) of intense pleasure. But the dramatic realities work against her most valiant efforts. For there is no respite, and, in her most lucid moments, the 'holy light' of Milton seems rather to be that of the 'hellish sun', which has already scorched the surrounding grass, which may be the cause of her parasol igniting, and which threatens to char her own flesh and that of her husband.

Winnie seeks comfort and reassurance primarily from the (token) presence of the crude and brutish Willie. She needs him as a witness to her own existence. But she needs him above all as someone to whom she can address the words that are so vital to her need to go on saying them, for 'as long as there are any'. For one of the most striking things about Winnie is her capacity to persuade herself that she can understand and assert control over reality, even though, intermittently and fleetingly, she becomes aware that a time will come when words must fail, that they will run out before the end is reached, that there will be no one left for them to address.

She also finds some degree of shared comfort in the literary quotations that she recites. Various drafts of the play indicate that these were chosen with great care by Beckett, not only for the ideas and emotions that they express, but also to ensure that they fall within her range of reference. Six of them figure, for example, in Bartlett's popular *Familiar Quotations,* while perhaps only one (the Charles Wolfe 'Song' from *The Burial of Sir John Moore and Other Poems*) is little known. Naturally, Winnie's 'classics' acquire deeper resonance if you happen to recognise the references, although these tend to be used functionally rather than allusively. They do not evoke a contrasting, richer civilisation, as T. S. Eliot might be said to have done in *The Waste Land,* but recall debris from a past culture in which Shakespeare, Herrick, Milton and Gray all seem to reveal the same sad truths about the human predicament, introducing, for instance (unnoticed, it would seem, by Winnie), 'woe' and the transitoriness of earthly things into her meditations. Dramatically speaking, Winnie's quotations enrich, as well as undercut, her own language.[3] But as her memory progressively fails, so the lines that she quotes appear in incorrect, fragmented or half-remembered form, and in the second act her well-tried formula, 'What are those immortal lines?', fails at times to trigger any recollection or recitation, however faltering.

Publication and production

Once the play was ready for production, there was a great deal of discussion as to where it should be premiered and who should play the very demanding role of Winnie. Beckett wanted it to be directed first by his friend Donald McWhinnie, for the Royal Court Theatre in London, in autumn 1961. He originally set his sights on Laurence Olivier's wife, Joan Plowright, to play Winnie, but this proved impossible on account of her pregnancy. Meanwhile, Alan Schneider was preparing to direct the play in New York. Schneider offered to delay the American production but Beckett declined his offer, with the result that *Happy Days* began its stage life at the Cherry Lane Theatre in New York on 17 September 1961. A talented American actress, Ruth White, inaugurated the role. Schneider had earlier directed the American premieres of *Waiting for Godot*, *Endgame* and *Krapp's Last Tape*. The published correspondence between director and author reveals how much detailed discussion of *Happy Days* took place by letter and by telephone: the appearance of the set, of the costumes, of Winnie herself and her partner, Willie.[4] It was mainly on account of the priority of the American production that the play was first published by Grove Press in New York at the end of 1961.

Soon after its completion, *Happy Days* was translated into German by Elmar and Erika Tophoven (with advice from Beckett, whose German was fluent) and produced only two weeks after the American premiere at the Schiller-Theater Werkstatt in Berlin, in late September 1961, with Berta Drews as Winnie. A British premiere was eventually mounted at the Royal Court Theatre in London in November 1962, directed by George Devine and assisted by Beckett. Brenda Bruce played Winnie, employing her natural Scottish accent. During the following year Beckett worked intensively with the French director Roger Blin and the distinguished actress Madeleine Renaud as Winnie, preparing the French premiere of *Oh les beaux jours* for the Odéon Théâtre de France in Paris, its title drawn from Verlaine's poem about two spectral figures, 'Colloque sentimental'.

Nearly a decade later, in 1971, Beckett was invited by the Schiller-Theater in Berlin to direct Eva Katharina Schultz in the German version, *Glückliche Tage*. He spent many weeks visualising the play, during which many of the small cuts and changes he made to the text were conceived and put into practice. Three years later, he came over to London to attend rehearsals for a production at the newly built National Theatre, directed by Peter Hall, with Dame Peggy Ashcroft as Winnie. Director and actress were in agreement in resisting some of Beckett's more radical cuts, such as the entire scene in which the parasol bursts dramatically into flames. But when Beckett came to London again to direct the play himself in 1979 at the Royal Court Theatre, with his favourite actress, Billie Whitelaw, he introduced only a few of these major cuts. Instead, he made numerous minor changes (described in detail in the *Happy Days* production notebook referred to earlier), largely of a single word or phrase (e.g. 'and now' for 'what now,' 'talk' for 'speak' and so on) which have a definite part to play in marking out the phases of Winnie's old-style 'day' and in helping to reinforce an intricate choreography of word and gesture through repetition, echo and musicality.

Critical reception

According to most accounts, Ruth White's performance as Winnie in the New York premiere in 1961 was outstanding ('extraordinary in its concentration, variety, nuance and endurance', *The Nation*, 7 October 1961), in a production which aimed to be as faithful as possible to Beckett's text and stage directions. The play itself was received with rather less enthusiasm. The *Village Voice* (21 September 1961) described it as 'thinner in texture, slighter in consequence than all its forerunners' and, even among those who found much to admire in it, the view was expressed that 'Beckett's metaphor was over-extended' (*Educational Theatre Journal*, 13, 1961) and that the play was essentially untheatrical. Yet there was also some understanding and sensitivity of response – again from Harold Clurman in *The Nation*, who wrote that Beckett's play was 'a poem for the stage, a poem of despair and forbearance . . . to wait and suffer, perhaps to hope and pray in the empty world, is to evince a trait of nobility, even of heroism'. John Gassner took a different view of the issue of heroism: 'Never yielding an inch to sentimentality, against which the writing defends itself with sustained irony, so that human heroism also appears to be a ridiculous capacity for self-delusion, *Happy Days* is compact and self-contained' (*Educational Theatre Journal*). Beckett himself would remain adamant that Winnie was largely unaware of the sad realities of her situation ('She's not stoic, she's unaware,' he said at a rehearsal in 1979),[5] and he reacted strongly against the notion that there was anything heroic about his heroine.[6]

Predictably enough, critical response to the play in Britain was varied, and reactions to Brenda Bruce's performance were mixed. For Milton Shulman in the *Evening Standard*, the entire evening proved to be a colossal bore – he blamed the author, however, who 'lacked intellectual fibre', and not the actress – whereas the anonymous *Times* drama critic (Irving Wardle) had serious reservations about Miss Bruce's performance, finding that the demands of Beckett's language defeated her, but felt that *Happy Days* might well prove to be as fiercely effective onstage as *Krapp's Last Tape*, remarking perceptively that what the play says 'is irreducibly contained in the shape of its sentences and in its dominant theatrical image . . . The text is an elaborate structure of internal harmonies, with recurring clichés twisted into bitter truths, and key phrases chiming ironically through the development as in a passacaglia' (*The Times*, 2 November 1962). Philip Hope-Wallace in the *Guardian* conceded that the play had a 'certain hypnotic power', and Bernard Levin in the *Daily Mail* expressed the view that Brenda Bruce's performance was a remarkable tour de force in a play that 'will haunt those who see it'. W. A. Darlington also praised Brenda Bruce's 'wonderfully expressive acting in a part of the utmost difficulty' (*Daily Telegraph*, 2 November 1962). The subsequent Dublin production of John Beary in September 1963 had a cheerier Winnie in the person of Marie Kean, the Irish actress, whose 'beautifully managed performance' (Philip Hope-Wallace in *The Guardian*) was judged to be more vivid than the earlier Royal Court production, particularly in the play's moments of terror and desolation. With her Irish lilt and range of vocal tones, Marie Kean seems to have given one of the more memorable performances in English of a role that presents a huge challenge even to the most accomplished actresses.

Certainly one of the most distinguished actresses to have played Winnie was Madeleine Renaud, who gave the first performance in French with her husband, the famous Jean-Louis Barrault, in the tiny role of Willie. The production was directed by Roger Blin in September and October 1963, with much help from Beckett. Renaud's interpretation derived recognisably from the French grand theatrical tradition, yet it had a delicacy and subtlety of shading rarely associated with the broader, more rhetorical manner of the traditional French style. After the production had been brought to London for a second run in 1969, Irving Wardle wrote of Madeleine Renaud's performance: 'The woman she presents is not the bluff, earthy figure familiar from English productions of the play. She is an emblem of middle-class decorum, holding the sense of chaos and despair at bay by reliance upon a fixed code of good manners and regular habits' (*The Times*, 27 September 1969). At its opening performances in 1963, Blin's production divided critics, although all were agreed as to the technical brilliance and poignancy of Madeleine Renaud. Jean-Jacques Gautier, habitually hostile to Beckett's work, described the play in *Le Figaro* as a repulsive 'festival d'abjection' ('a festival of abasement') and an 'apothéose du néant' ('apotheosis of nothingness'), while Elsa Triolet (the wife of Louis Aragon) was

xiv

prompted in *Les Lettres françaises* to a strongly worded affirmation of life – in the face of a work which she regarded as truly
'atroce' ('dreadful'). Pascal, the Book of Job and the figure of
Prometheus were all invoked by Gilles Sandier in a lengthy
review of the play in *Arts*, in which *Oh les beaux jours* was
favourably compared with Claudel's epic historical drama *Le
Soulier de Satin*.

Madeleine Renaud's performance as Winnie has been the
most familiar and most prestigious of all the European productions, not least for being performed in so many countries –
including Italy, Switzerland, Yugoslavia, Britain and America.
The American tour provided New York audiences with an
opportunity to compare the French and American performances, Madeleine Renaud alternating at the Cherry Lane
Theatre with Ruth White. Harold Clurman found that
Madeleine Renaud produced a superbly accomplished 'remem-
bered performance', classically French, but lacked some of the
freshness, spontaneity and humanity of Ruth White (*Nation*,
201, 18 October 1965). Madeleine Renaud certainly projected a
serene, lyrical and moving Winnie, with which not everyone
would agree, and her view of the play as 'une pièce d'amour' ('a
play about love') might seem a pale, unduly optimistic reading.

There have been a number of striking later productions of
Happy Days involving Billie Whitelaw, Irene Worth, Natasha
Parry (acted in French and directed by Peter Brook); more
recently, Felicity Kendal (directed by Sir Peter Hall) and
Rosaleen Linehan in Karel Reisz's production for Dublin's Gate
Theatre. Fiona Shaw, in a production which began life at the
National Theatre's Lyttelton Theatre in London in January
2007, was placed in front of a large painting of a desolate desert,
on a wide stage littered with huge blocks of stone and concrete,
evoking an apocalyptic vision that reminded *The Stage*'s critic of
'some Middle Eastern bunker' and others of an urban landscape after a nuclear holocaust. There have been many variants
on the 'expanse of scorched grass rising centre to low mound'
described in the opening stage direction. Some have been

experimental and eccentric, others wild: a mound resembling a bale of hay, a rocky promontory, a pile of cardboard boxes. Those that have been most effective have tended to be closest to the 'maximum of simplicity and symmetry' of Beckett's stage directions and to have focused without needless distraction on the brightly lit figure of Winnie in the 'exact centre of mound'.

Happy Days has by now taken its place with *Waiting for Godot*, *Endgame* and *Krapp's Last Tape* among the canonical dramas of the twentieth century. Perhaps Beckett's most impressive achievement is to have created an ordinary middle-class woman, a creature of habit par excellence, able to speak only in commonplaces, and yet to have made from this a work of searing power: a play that recalls, as one French critic put it, 'the immobility of the great sacred theatrical works, in which human speech sufficed to fill and animate the theatrical space, and which consisted entirely of the essential realities to which these texts return one: Time, Space, and the Word'.[7]

James Knowlson

Notes

1 Ruby Cohn, *The Comic Gamut* (New Brunswick, NJ: Rutgers University Press, 1962), p. 257.

2 Samuel Beckett speaking at a rehearsal of *Happy Days* in London in 1979; recorded by Martha Dow Fehsenfeld and cited in *Happy Days: The Production Notebook of Samuel Beckett*, ed. James Knowlson (London: Faber and Faber, 1985), p. 17.

3 Ruby Cohn, *Back to Beckett* (Princeton, NJ: Princeton University Press), p. 181.

4 Maurice Harmon (ed.), *No Author Better Served: The Correspondence of Samuel Beckett and Alan Schneider* (Boston, Mass.: Harvard University Press, 1998).

5 *Happy Days: The Production Notebook of Samuel Beckett*, p.17.

6 Samuel Beckett in conversation with James Knowlson at the Hyde Park Hotel, London, May 1979.

7 Gilles Sandier, *Arts*, 935, 6–12 November 1963.

Table of Dates

Where unspecified, translations from French to English or vice versa are by Beckett.

1906

13 April — Samuel Beckett [Samuel Barclay Beckett] born in 'Cooldrinagh', a house in Foxrock, a village south of Dublin, on Good Friday, the second child of William Beckett and May Beckett, née Roe; he is preceded by a brother, Frank Edward, born 26 July 1902.

1911

Enters kindergarten at Ida and Pauline Elsner's private academy in Leopardstown.

1915

Attends larger Earlsfort House School in Dublin.

1920

Follows Frank to Portora Royal, a distinguished Protestant boarding school in Enniskillen, County Fermanagh (soon to become part of Northern Ireland).

1923

October — Enrols at Trinity College Dublin (TCD) to study for an Arts degree.

1926

August — First visit to France, a month-long cycling tour of the Loire Valley.

1927

April–August — Travels through Florence and Venice, visiting museums, galleries and churches.

December — Receives BA in Modern Languages (French and Italian) and graduates first in the First Class.

1933

3 May	Death of Peggy Sinclair from tuberculosis.
26 June	Death of William Beckett from a heart attack.

1934

January	Moves to London and begins psychoanalysis with Wilfred Bion at the Tavistock Clinic.
February	*Negro Anthology*, edited by Nancy Cunard and with numerous translations by Beckett from the French (London: Wishart & Co.).
May	*More Pricks Than Kicks* (London: Chatto & Windus).
Aug.–Sept.	Contributes several stories and reviews to literary magazines in London and Dublin.

1935

November	*Echo's Bones and Other Precipitates*, a cycle of thirteen poems (Paris: Europa Press).

1936

	Returns to Dublin.
29 September	Leaves Ireland for a seven-month stay in Germany.

1937

Apr.–Aug.	First serious attempt at a play, *Human Wishes*, about Samuel Johnson and his household.
October	Settles in Paris.

1938

6/7 January	Stabbed by a street pimp in Montparnasse. Among his visitors at Hôpital Broussais is Suzanne Deschevaux-Dumesnil, an acquaintance who is to become Beckett's companion for life.
March	*Murphy* (London: Routledge).
April	Begins writing poetry directly in French.

1939

3 September	Great Britain and France declare war on Germany. Beckett abruptly ends a visit to Ireland and returns to Paris the next day.

1940

June — Travels south with Suzanne following the Fall of France, as part of the exodus from the capital.

September — Returns to Paris.

1941

13 January — Death of James Joyce in Zurich.

1 September — Joins the Resistance cell Gloria SMH.

1942

16 August — Goes into hiding with Suzanne after the arrest of close friend Alfred Péron.

6 October — Arrival at Roussillon, a small village in unoccupied southern France.

1944

24 August — Liberation of Paris.

1945

30 March — Awarded the Croix de Guerre.

Aug.–Dec. — Volunteers as a storekeeper and interpreter with the Irish Red Cross in Saint-Lô, Normandy.

1946

July — Publishes first fiction in French – a truncated version of the short story 'Suite' (later to become 'La Fin') in *Les Temps modernes*, owing to a misunderstanding by editors – as well as a critical essay on Dutch painters Geer and Bram van Velde in *Cahiers d'art*.

1947

Jan.–Feb. — Writes first play, in French, *Eleutheria* (published posthumously).

April — *Murphy*, French translation (Paris: Bordas).

1948

Undertakes a number of translations commissioned by UNESCO and by Georges Duthuit.

1950

25 August   Death of May Beckett.

1951

March   *Molloy*, in French (Paris: Les Éditions de Minuit).

November   *Malone meurt* (Paris: Minuit).

1952

Purchases land at Ussy-sur-Marne, subsequently Beckett's preferred location for writing.

September   *En attendant Godot* (Paris: Minuit).

1953

5 January   Premiere of *Godot* at the Théâtre de Babylone in Montparnasse, directed by Roger Blin.

May   *L'Innommable* (Paris: Minuit).

August   *Watt*, in English (Paris: Olympia Press).

1954

8 September   *Waiting for Godot* (New York: Grove Press).

13 September   Death of Frank Beckett from lung cancer.

1955

March   *Molloy*, translated into English with Patrick Bowles (New York: Grove; Paris: Olympia).

3 August   First English production of *Godot* opens in London at the Arts Theatre.

November   *Nouvelles et Textes pour rien* (Paris: Minuit).

1956

3 January   American *Godot* premiere in Miami.

February   First British publication of *Waiting for Godot* (London: Faber).

October   *Malone Dies* (New York: Grove).

1957

January   First radio broadcast, *All That Fall* on the BBC Third Programme.

Fin de partie, suivi de Acte sans paroles (Paris: Minuit).

28 March   Death of Jack B. Yeats.

May	Assists with the German production of *Play* (*Spiel*, translated by Elmar and Erika Tophoven) in Ulm.
22 May	Outline of *Film* sent to Grove Press. *Film* would be produced in 1964, starring Buster Keaton, and released at the Venice Film Festival the following year.
1964	
March	*Play and Two Short Pieces for Radio* (London: Faber).
April	*How It Is*, translation of *Comment c'est* (London: Calder; New York: Grove).
June	*Comédie*, translation of *Play*, in *Les Lettres nouvelles*.
July–Aug.	First and only trip to the United States, to assist with the production of *Film* in New York.
1965	
October	*Imagination morte imaginez* (Paris: Minuit).
November	*Imagination Dead Imagine* (London: *The Sunday Times*; Calder).
1966	
January	*Comédie et Actes divers*, including *Dis Joe* and *Va et vient* (Paris: Minuit).
February	*Assez* (Paris: Minuit).
October	*Bing* (Paris: Minuit).
1967	
February	*D'un ouvrage abandonné* (Paris: Minuit). *Têtes-mortes* (Paris: Minuit).
16 March	Death of Thomas MacGreevy.
June	*Eh Joe and Other Writings*, including *Act Without Words II* and *Film* (London: Faber).
July	*Come and Go*, English translation of *Va et vient* (London: Calder).
26 September	Directs first solo production, *Endspiel* (translation of *Endgame* by Elmar Tophoven) in Berlin.

November	*No's Knife: Collected Shorter Prose, 1945–1966* (London: Calder).
December	*Stories and Texts for Nothing*, illustrated with six ink line drawings by Avigdor Arikha (New York: Grove).
1968	
March	*Poèmes* (Paris: Minuit).
December	*Watt*, translated into French with Ludovic and Agnès Janvier (Paris: Minuit).
1969	
23 October	Awarded the Nobel Prize for Literature. *Sans* (Paris: Minuit).
1970	
April	*Mercier et Camier* (Paris: Minuit). *Premier amour* (Paris: Minuit).
July	*Lessness*, translation of *Sans* (London: Calder).
September	*Le Dépeupleur* (Paris: Minuit).
1972	
January	*The Lost Ones*, translation of *Le Dépeupleur* (London: Calder; New York: Grove). *The North*, part of *The Lost Ones*, illustrated with etchings by Arikha (London: Enitharmon Press).
1973	
January	*Not I* (London: Faber).
July	*First Love* (London: Calder).
1974	
	Mercier and Camier (London: Calder).
1975	
Spring	Directs *Godot* in Berlin and *Pas moi* (translation of *Not I*) in Paris.
1976	
February	*Pour finir encore et autres foirades* (Paris: Minuit).
20 May	Directs Billie Whitelaw in *Footfalls*, which is performed with *That Time* at London's Royal

	production of *Godot*, directed by Walter Asmus, in London.
	Collected Shorter Plays (London: Faber; New York: Grove).
May	*Collected Poems, 1930–1978* (London: Calder).
July	*Collected Shorter Prose, 1945–1980* (London: Calder).
1989	
April	*Stirrings Still*, with illustrations by Louis le Brocquy (New York: Blue Moon Books).
June	*Nohow On: Company, Ill Seen Ill Said, Worstward Ho*, illustrated with etchings by Robert Ryman (New York: Limited Editions Club).
17 July	Death of Suzanne Beckett.
22 December	Death of Samuel Beckett. Burial in Cimetière de Montparnasse.

★

1990	
	As the Story Was Told: Uncollected and Late Prose (London: Calder; New York: Riverrun Press).
1992	
	Dream of Fair to Middling Women (Dublin: Black Cat Press).
1995	
	Eleutheria (Paris: Minuit).
1996	
	Eleutheria, translated into English by Barbara Wright (London: Faber).
1998	
	No Author Better Served: The Correspondence of Samuel Beckett and Alan Schneider, edited by Maurice Harmon (Cambridge, Mass.: Harvard University Press).

Compiled by Cassandra Nelson

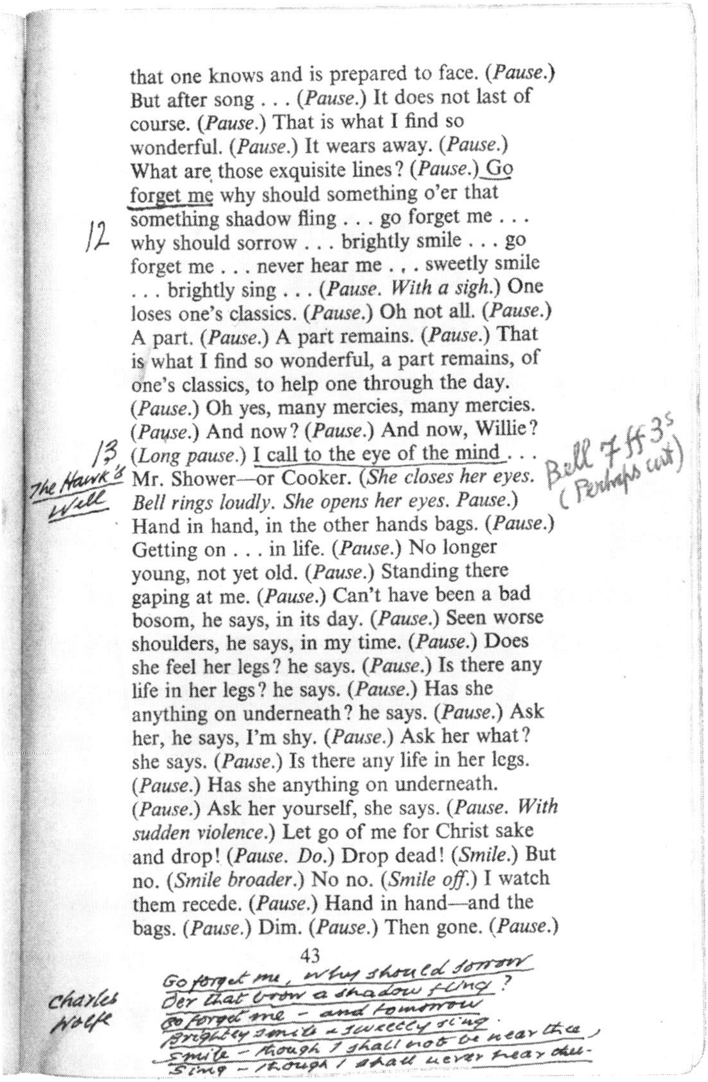

that one knows and is prepared to face. (*Pause.*)
But after song . . . (*Pause.*) It does not last of
course. (*Pause.*) That is what I find so
wonderful. (*Pause.*) It wears away. (*Pause.*)
What are those exquisite lines? (*Pause.*) <u>Go
forget me</u> why should something o'er that
something shadow fling . . . go forget me . . .
why should sorrow . . . brightly smile . . . go
forget me . . . never hear me . . . sweetly smile
. . . brightly sing . . . (*Pause. With a sigh.*) One
loses one's classics. (*Pause.*) Oh not all. (*Pause.*)
A part. (*Pause.*) A part remains. (*Pause.*) That
is what I find so wonderful, a part remains, of
one's classics, to help one through the day.
(*Pause.*) Oh yes, many mercies, many mercies.
(*Pause.*) And now? (*Pause.*) And now, Willie?
(*Long pause.*) <u>I call to the eye of the mind</u> . . .
Mr. Shower—or Cooker. (*She closes her eyes.*)
Bell rings loudly. She opens her eyes. Pause.)
Hand in hand, in the other hands bags. (*Pause.*)
Getting on . . . in life. (*Pause.*) No longer
young, not yet old. (*Pause.*) Standing there
gaping at me. (*Pause.*) Can't have been a bad
bosom, he says, in its day. (*Pause.*) Seen worse
shoulders, he says, in my time. (*Pause.*) Does
she feel her legs? he says. (*Pause.*) Is there any
life in her legs? he says. (*Pause.*) Has she
anything on underneath? he says. (*Pause.*) Ask
her, he says, I'm shy. (*Pause.*) Ask her what?
she says. (*Pause.*) Is there any life in her legs.
(*Pause.*) Has she anything on underneath.
(*Pause.*) Ask her yourself, she says. (*Pause. With
sudden violence.*) Let go of me for Christ sake
and drop! (*Pause. Do.*) Drop dead! (*Smile.*) But
no. (*Smile broader.*) No no. (*Smile off.*) I watch
them recede. (*Pause.*) Hand in hand—and the
bags. (*Pause.*) Dim. (*Pause.*) Then gone. (*Pause.*)

43

[handwritten annotations in margins:]

12

13
The Hawk's Well

Bell 7 ff 3s
(Perhaps cut)

Charles Wolfe

Go forget me, why should sorrow
O'er that brow a shadow fling?
Go forget me — and tomorrow
Brightly smile & sweetly sing.
Smile — though I shall not be near thee,
Sing — though I shall never hear thee.

Beckett's annotated copy of *Happy Days*, prepared for his
production of the play at the Old Vic, London, 1975.
Courtesy of the Beckett International Foundation, University of Reading.
© The Estate of Samuel Beckett.

Happy Days

CHARACTERS

WINNIE   *a woman of about fifty*
WILLIE   *a man of about sixty*

Act One

Expanse of scorched grass rising centre to low mound. Gentle slopes down to front and either side of stage. Back an abrupter fall to stage level. Maximum of simplicity and symmetry.

Blazing light.

Very pompier trompe-l'oeil backcloth to represent unbroken plain and sky receding to meet in far distance.

Embedded up to above her waist in exact centre of mound, WINNIE. *About fifty, well-preserved, blonde for preference, plump, arms and shoulders bare, low bodice, big bosom, pearl necklace. She is discovered sleeping, her arms on the ground before her, her head on her arms. Beside her on ground to her left a capacious black bag, shopping variety, and to her right a collapsible collapsed parasol, beak of handle emerging from sheath.*

To her right and rear, lying asleep on ground, hidden by mound, WILLIE.

Long pause. A bell rings piercingly, say ten seconds, stops. She does not move. Pause. Bell more piercingly, say five seconds. She wakes. Bell stops. She raises her head, gazes front. Long pause. She straightens up, lays her hands flat on ground, throws back her head and gazes at zenith. Long pause.

WINNIE: [*Gazing at zenith.*] Another heavenly day. [*Pause. Head back level, eyes front, pause. She clasps hands to breast, closes eyes. Lips move in inaudible prayer, say ten seconds. Lips still. Hands remain clasped. Low.*] For Jesus Christ sake Amen. [*Eyes open, hands unclasp, return to mound. Pause. She clasps hands to breast again, closes eyes, lips move again in inaudible addendum, say five seconds. Low.*] World without end Amen. [*Eyes open, hands unclasp, return to mound. Pause.*] Begin, Winnie. [*Pause.*] Begin your day, Winnie. [*Pause. She turns to bag, rummages in it without*

5

*moving it from its place, brings out toothbrush, rummages
again, brings out flat tube of toothpaste, turns back front,
unscrews cap of tube, lays cap on ground, squeezes with
difficulty small blob of paste on brush, holds tube in one hand
and brushes teeth with other. She turns modestly aside and
back to her right to spit out behind mound. In this position
her eyes rest on* WILLIE. *She spits out. She cranes a little
farther back and down. Loud.*] Hoo-oo! [*Pause. Louder.*]
Hoo-oo! [*Pause. Tender smile as she turns back front, lays
down brush.*] Poor Willie – [*examines tube, smile off*] –
running out – [*looks for cap*] – ah well – [*finds cap*] –
can't be helped – [*screws on cap*] – just one of those old
things – [*lays down tube*] – another of those old things –
[*turns towards bag*] – just can't be cured – [*rummages in
bag*] – cannot be cured – [*brings out small mirror, turns
back front*] – ah yes – [*inspects teeth in mirror*] – poor dear
Willie – [*testing upper front teeth with thumb, indistinctly*] –
good Lord! – [*pulling back upper lip to inspect gums, do.*] –
good God! – [*pulling back corner of mouth, mouth open,
do.*] – ah well – [*other corner, do.*] – no worse – [*abandons
inspection, normal speech*] – no better, no worse – [*lays
down mirror*] – no change – [*wipes fingers on grass*] – no
pain – [*looks for toothbrush*] – hardly any – [*takes up
toothbrush*] – great thing that – [*examines handle of brush*]
– nothing like it – [*examines handle, reads*] – pure . . .
what? – [*pause*] – what? – [*lays down brush*] – ah yes –
[*turns towards bag*] – poor Willie – [*rummages in bag*] – no
zest – [*rummages*] – for anything – [*brings out spectacles in
case*] – no interest – [*turns back front*] – in life – [*takes
spectacles from case*] – poor dear Willie – [*lays down case*] –
sleep for ever – [*opens spectacles*] – marvellous gift – [*puts
on spectacles*] – nothing to touch it – [*looks for toothbrush*]
– in my opinion – [*takes up toothbrush*] – always said so –
[*examines handle of brush*] – wish I had it – [*examines
handle, reads*] – genuine . . . pure . . . what? – [*lays down
brush*] – blind next – [*takes off spectacles*] – ah well – [*lays

down spectacles] – seen enough – [*feels in bodice for handkerchief*] – I suppose – [*takes out folded handkerchief*] – by now – [*shakes out handkerchief*] – what are those wonderful lines – [*wipes one eye*] – woe woe is me – [*wipes the other*] – to see what I see – [*looks for spectacles*] – ah yes – [*takes up spectacles*] – wouldn't miss it – [*starts polishing spectacles, breathing on lenses*] – or would I? – [*polishes*] – holy light – [*polishes*] – bob up out of dark – [*polishes*] – blaze of hellish light. [*Stops polishing, raises face to sky, pause, head back level, resumes polishing, stops polishing, cranes back to her right and down.*] Hoo-oo! [*Pause. Tender smile as she turns back front and resumes polishing. Smile off.*] Marvellous gift – [*stops polishing, lays down spectacles*] – wish I had it – [*folds handkerchief*] – ah well – [*puts handkerchief back in bodice*] – can't complain – [*looks for spectacles*] – no no – [*takes up spectacles*] – mustn't complain – [*holds up spectacles, looks through lens*] – so much to be thankful for – [*looks through other lens*] – no pain – [*puts on spectacles*] – hardly any – [*looks for toothbrush*] – wonderful thing that – [*takes up toothbrush*] – nothing like it – [*examines handle of brush*] – slight headache sometimes – [*examines handle, reads*] – guaranteed . . . genuine . . . pure . . . what? – [*looks closer*] – genuine pure   – [*takes handkerchief from bodice*] – ah yes – [*shakes out handkerchief*] – occasional mild migraine – [*starts wiping handle of brush*] – it comes – [*wipes*] – then goes – [*wiping mechanically*] – ah yes – [*wiping*] – many mercies – [*wiping*] – great mercies – [*stops wiping, fixed lost gaze, brokenly*] – prayers perhaps not for naught – [*pause, do.*] – first thing – [*pause, do.*] – last thing – [*head down, resumes wiping, stops wiping, head up, calmed, wipes eyes, folds handkerchief, puts it back in bodice, examines handle of brush, reads*] – fully guaranteed . . . genuine pure . . . – [*looks closer*] – genuine pure . . . [*Takes off spectacles, lays them and brush down, gazes before her.*] Old things. [*Pause.*] Old eyes. [*Long pause.*] On,

Winnie. [*She casts about her, sees parasol, considers it at length, takes it up and develops from sheath a handle of surprising length. Holding butt of parasol in right hand she cranes back and down to her right to hang over* WILLIE.] Hoo-oo! [*Pause.*] Willie! [*Pause.*] Wonderful gift. [*She strikes down at him with beak of parasol.*] Wish I had it. [*She strikes again. The parasol slips from her grasp and falls behind mound. It is immediately restored to her by* WILLIE'S *invisible hand.*] Thank you, dear. [*She transfers parasol to left hand, turns back front and examines right palm.*] Damp. [*Returns parasol to right hand, examines left palm.*] Ah well, no worse. [*Head up, cheerfully.*] No better, no worse, no change. [*Pause. Do.*] No pain. [*Cranes back to look down at* WILLIE, *holding parasol by butt as before.*] Don't go off on me again now dear will you please, I may need you. [*Pause.*] No hurry, no hurry, just don't curl up on me again. [*Turns back front, lays down parasol, examines palms together, wipes them on grass.*] Perhaps a shade off colour just the same. [*Turns to bag, rummages in it, brings out revolver, holds it up, kisses it rapidly, puts it back, rummages, brings out almost empty bottle of red medicine, turns back front, looks for spectacles, puts them on, reads label.*] Loss of spirits . . . lack of keenness . . . want of appetite . . . infants . . . children . . . adults . . . six level . . . tablespoonfuls daily – [*head up, smile*] – the old style! – [*smile off, head down, reads*] – daily . . . before and after . . . meals . . . instantaneous . . . [*looks closer*] . . . improvement. [*Takes off spectacles, lays them down, holds up bottle at arm's length to see level, unscrews cap, swigs it off head well back, tosses cap and bottle away in* WILLIE'S *direction. Sound of breaking glass.*] Ah that's better! [*Turns to bag, rummages in it, brings out lipstick, turns back front, examines lipstick.*] Running out. [*Looks for spectacles.*] Ah well. [*Puts on spectacles, looks for mirror.*] Mustn't complain. [*Takes up mirror, starts doing lips.*] What is that wonderful line? [*Lips.*] Oh fleeting joys – [*lips*] – oh

8

something lasting woe. [*Lips. She is interrupted by disturbance from* WILLIE. *He is sitting up. She lowers lipstick and mirror and cranes back and down to look at him. Pause. Top back of* WILLIE's *bald head, trickling blood, rises to view above slope, comes to rest.* WINNIE *pushes up her spectacles. Pause. His hand appears with handkerchief, spreads it on skull, disappears. Pause. The hand appears with boater, club ribbon, settles it on head, rakish angle, disappears. Pause.* WINNIE *cranes a little further back and down.*] Slip on your drawers, dear, before you get singed. [*Pause.*] No? [*Pause.*] Oh I see, you still have some of that stuff left. [*Pause.*] Work it well in, dear. [*Pause.*] Now the other. [*Pause. She turns back front, gazes before her. Happy expression.*] Oh this is going to be another happy day! [*Pause. Happy expression off. She pulls down spectacles and resumes lips.* WILLIE *opens newspaper, hands invisible. Tops of yellow sheets appear on either side of his head.* WINNIE *finishes lips, inspects them in mirror held a little further away.*] Ensign crimson. [WILLIE *turns page.* WINNIE *lays down lipstick and mirror, turns towards bag.*] Pale flag. [WILLIE *turns page.* WINNIE *rummages in bag, brings out small ornate brimless hat with crumpled feather, turns back front, straightens hat, smooths feather, raises it towards head, arrests gesture as* WILLIE *reads.*]

WILLIE: His Grace and Most Reverend Father in God Dr Carolus Hunter dead in tub.

[*Pause.*]

WINNIE: [*Gazing front, hat in hand, tone of fervent reminiscence.*] Charlie Hunter! [*Pause.*] I close my eyes – [*she takes off spectacles and does so, hat in one hand, spectacles in other,* WILLIE *turns page*] – and am sitting on his knees again, in the back garden at Borough Green, under the horse-beech. [*Pause. She opens eyes, puts on spectacles, fiddles with hat.*] Oh the happy memories! [*Pause. She raises hat towards head, arrests gesture as* WILLIE *reads.*]

9

WILLIE: Opening for smart youth.

[*Pause. She raises hat towards head, arrests gesture, takes off spectacles, gazes front, hat in one hand, spectacles in other.*]

WINNIE: My first ball! [*Long pause.*] My second ball! [*Long pause. Closes eyes.*] My first kiss! [*Pause.* WILLIE *turns page.* WINNIE *opens eyes.*] A Mr Johnson, or Johnston, or perhaps I should say John*stone.* Very bushy moustache, very tawny. [*Reverently.*] Almost ginger! [*Pause.*] Within a toolshed, though whose I cannot conceive. We had no toolshed and he most certainly had no toolshed. [*Closes eyes.*] I see the piles of pots. [*Pause.*] The tangles of bast. [*Pause.*] The shadows deepening among the rafters. [*Pause. She opens eyes, puts on spectacles, raises hat towards head, arrests gesture as* WILLIE *reads.*]

WILLIE: Wanted bright boy.

[*Pause.* WINNIE *puts on hat hurriedly, looks for mirror.* WILLIE *turns page.* WINNIE *takes up mirror, inspects hat, lays down mirror, turns towards bag. Paper disappears.* WINNIE *rummages in bag, brings out magnifying-glass, turns back front, looks for toothbrush. Paper reappears, folded, and begins to fan* WILLIE'S *face, hand invisible.* WINNIE *takes up toothbrush and examines handle through glass.*]

WINNIE: Fully guaranteed . . . [WILLIE *stops fanning*] . . . genuine pure . . . [*Pause.* WILLIE *resumes fanning.* WINNIE *looks closer, reads.*] Fully guaranteed . . . [WILLIE *stops fanning*] . . . genuine pure . . . [*Pause.* WILLIE *resumes fanning.* WINNIE *lays down glass and brush, takes handkerchief from bodice, takes off and polishes spectacles, puts on spectacles, looks for glass, takes up and polishes glass, lays down glass, looks for brush, takes up brush and wipes handle, lays down brush, puts handkerchief back in bodice, looks for glass, takes up glass, looks for brush, takes up brush and examines handle through glass.*] Fully guaranteed . . . [WILLIE *stops fanning*] . . . genuine pure . . . [*pause,* WILLIE *resumes fanning*] . . . hog's . . . [WILLIE *stops fanning, pause*] . . . setae. [*Pause.* WINNIE *lays down glass and brush, paper disappears,* WINNIE *takes off spectacles, lays them down, gazes front.*] Hog's setae. [*Pause.*] That is what I find so wonderful, that not a day goes by – [*smile*] – to speak in the old style – [*smile off*] – hardly a day, without some addition to one's knowledge however trifling, the addition I mean, provided one takes the pains. [WILLIE'*s hand reappears with a postcard which he examines close to eyes.*] And if for some strange reason no further pains are possible, why then just close the eyes – [*she does so*] – and wait for the day to come – [*opens eyes*] – the happy day to come when flesh melts at so many degrees and the night of the moon has so many hundred hours. [*Pause.*] That is what I find so comforting when I lose heart and envy the brute beast. [*Turning towards* WILLIE.] I hope you are taking in – [*She sees postcard, bends lower.*] What is that you have there, Willie, may I see? [*She reaches down with hand and* WILLIE *hands her card. The hairy forearm appears above slope, raised in gesture of giving, the hand open to take back, and remains in this position till card is returned.* WINNIE *turns back front and examines card.*] Heavens what are they up to! [*She looks for spectacles, puts them on and examines card.*] No but this is just genuine pure filth! [*Examines card.*] Make any nice-minded person want to vomit! [*Impatience of* WILLIE'*s fingers. She looks for glass, takes it up and examines card through glass. Long pause.*] What does that creature in the background think he's doing? [*Looks closer.*] Oh no really! [*Impatience of fingers. Last long look. She lays down glass, takes edge of card between right forefinger and thumb, averts head, takes nose between left forefinger and thumb.*] Pah! [*Drops card.*] Take it away! [WILLIE'*s arm disappears. His hand reappears immediately, holding card.* WINNIE *takes off spectacles, lays them down, gazes before her. During what follows* WILLIE *continues to relish card, varying angles and distance from his eyes.*] Hog's setae. [*Puzzled expression.*] What exactly is a hog? [*Pause. Do.*] A sow of course I know, but a hog . . .

[*Puzzled expression off.*] Oh well what does it matter, that is what I always say, it will come back, that is what I find so wonderful, all comes back. [*Pause.*] All? [*Pause.*] No, not all. [*Smile.*] No no. [*Smile off.*] Not quite. [*Pause.*] A part. [*Pause.*] Floats up, one fine day, out of the blue. [*Pause.*] That is what I find so wonderful. [*Pause. She turns towards bag. Hand and card disappear. She makes to rummage in bag, arrests gesture.*] No. [*She turns back front. Smile.*] No no. [*Smile off.*] Gently Winnie. [*She gazes front.* WILLIE'*s hand reappears, takes off hat, disappears with hat.*] What then? [*Hand reappears, takes handkerchief from skull, disappears with handkerchief. Sharply, as to one not paying attention.*] Winnie! [WILLIE *bows head out of sight.*] What *is* the alternative? [*Pause.*] What *is* the al – [WILLIE *blows nose loud and long, head and hands invisible. She turns to look at him. Pause. Head reappears. Pause. Hand reappears with handkerchief, spreads it on skull, disappears. Pause. Hand reappears with boater, settles it on head, rakish angle, disappears. Pause.*] Would I had let you sleep on. [*She turns back front. Intermittent plucking at grass, head up and down, to animate following.*] Ah yes, if only I could bear to be alone, I mean prattle away with not a soul to hear. [*Pause.*] Not that I flatter myself you hear much, no Willie, God forbid. [*Pause.*] Days perhaps when you hear nothing. [*Pause.*] But days too when you answer. [*Pause.*] So that I may say at all times, even when you do not answer and perhaps hear nothing, something of this is being heard, I am not merely talking to myself, that is in the wilderness, a thing I could never bear to do – for any length of time. [*Pause.*] That is what enables me to go on, go on talking that is. [*Pause.*] Whereas if you were to die – [*smile*] – to speak in the old style – [*smile off*] – or go away and leave me, then what would I do, what *could* I do, all day long, I mean between the bell for waking and the bell for sleep? [*Pause.*] Simply gaze before me with compressed lips. [*Long pause while she does so. No more*

plucking.] Not another word as long as I drew breath,
nothing to break the silence of this place. [*Pause.*] Save
possibly, now and then, every now and then, a sigh into
my looking-glass. [*Pause.*] Or a brief . . . gale of laughter,
should I happen to see the old joke again. [*Pause. Smile
appears, broadens and seems about to culminate in laugh
when suddenly replaced by expression of anxiety.*] My hair!
[*Pause.*] Did I brush and comb my hair? [*Pause.*] I may
have done. [*Pause.*] Normally I do. [*Pause.*] There is so
little one *can* do. [*Pause.*] One does it all. [*Pause.*] All one
can. [*Pause.*] 'Tis only human. [*Pause.*] Human nature.
[*She begins to inspect mound, looks up.*] Human weakness.
[*She resumes inspection of mound, looks up.*] Natural
weakness. [*She resumes inspection of mound.*] I see no
comb. [*Inspects.*] Nor any hairbrush. [*Looks up. Puzzled
expression. She turns to bag, rummages in it.*] The comb is
here. [*Back front. Puzzled expression. Back to bag.
Rummages.*] The brush is here. [*Back front. Puzzled
expression.*] Perhaps I put them back, after use. [*Pause.
Do.*] But normally I do not put things back, after use, no,
I leave them lying about and put them back all together,
at the end of the day. [*Smile.*] To speak in the old style.
[*Pause.*] The sweet old style. [*Smile off.*] And yet . . . I
seem . . . to remember . . . [*Suddenly careless.*] Oh well,
what does it matter, that is what I always say, I shall
simply brush and comb them later on, purely and simply,
I have the whole – [*Pause. Puzzled.*] Them? [*Pause.*] Or it?
[*Pause.*] Brush and comb it? [*Pause.*] Sounds improper
somehow. [*Pause. Turning a little towards* WILLIE.] What
would you say, Willie? [*Pause. Turning a little further.*]
What would you say, Willie, speaking of your hair, them
or it? [*Pause.*] The hair on your head, I mean. [*Pause.
Turning a little further.*] The hair on your head, Willie,
what would you say speaking of the hair on your head,
them or it? [*Long pause.*]

WILLIE: It.

WINNIE: [*Turning back front, joyful.*] Oh you are going to talk
to me today, this is going to be a happy day! [*Pause. Joy
off.*] Another happy day. [*Pause.*] Ah well, where was I,
my hair, yes, later on, I shall be thankful for it later on.
[*Pause.*] I have my – [*raises hands to hat*] – yes, on, my hat
on – [*lowers hands*] – I cannot take it off now. [*Pause.*] To
think there are times one cannot take off one's hat, not if
one's life were at stake. Times one cannot put it on, times
one cannot take it off. [*Pause.*] How often I have said,
Put on your hat now, Winnie, there is nothing else for it,
take off your hat now, Winnie, like a good girl, it will do
you good, and did not. [*Pause.*] Could not. [*Pause. She
raises hand, frees a strand of hair from under hat, draws it
towards eye, squints at it, lets it go, hand down.*] Golden you
called it, that day, when the last guest was gone – [*hand
up in gesture of raising a glass*] – to your golden . . . may it
never . . . [*voice breaks*] . . . may it never . . . [*Hand down.
Head down. Pause. Low.*] That day. [*Pause. Do.*] What day?
[*Pause. Head up. Normal voice.*] What now? [*Pause.*] Words
fail, there are times when even they fail. [*Turning a little
towards* WILLIE.] Is that not so, Willie? [*Pause. Turning a
little further.*] Is not that so, Willie, that even words fail, at
times? [*Pause. Back front.*] What is one to do then, until
they come again? Brush and comb the hair, if it has not
been done, or if there is some doubt, trim the nails if
they are in need of trimming, these things tide one over.
[*Pause.*] That is what I mean. [*Pause.*] That is all I mean.
[*Pause.*] That is what I find so wonderful, that not a day
goes by – [*smile*] – to speak in the old style – [*smile off*] –
without some blessing – [WILLIE *collapses behind slope,
his head disappears,* WINNIE *turns towards event*] – in
disguise. [*She cranes back and down.*] Go back into your
hole now, Willie, you've exposed yourself enough.
[*Pause.*] Do as I say, Willie, don't lie sprawling there in
this hellish sun, go back into your hole. [*Pause.*] Go on
now, Willie. [WILLIE *invisible starts crawling left towards*

hole.] That's the man. [*She follows his progress with her eyes.*] Not head first, stupid, how are you going to turn? [*Pause.*] That's it . . . right round . . . now . . . back in. [*Pause.*] Oh I know it is not easy, dear, crawling backwards, but it is rewarding in the end. [*Pause.*] You have left your vaseline behind. [*She watches as he crawls back for vaseline.*] The lid! [*She watches as he crawls back towards hole. Irritated.*] Not head first, I tell you! [*Pause.*] More to the right. [*Pause.*] The *right*, I said. [*Pause. Irritated.*] Keep your tail down, can't you! [*Pause.*] Now. [*Pause.*] There! [*All these directions loud. Now in her normal voice, still turned towards him.*] Can you hear me? [*Pause.*] I beseech you, Willie, just yes or no, can you hear me, just yes or nothing.

[*Pause.*]

WILLIE: Yes.

WINNIE: [*Turning front, same voice.*] And now?

WILLIE: [*Irritated.*] Yes.

WINNIE: [*Less loud.*] And now?

WILLIE: [*More irritated.*] Yes.

WINNIE: [*Still less loud.*] And now? [*A little louder.*] And now?

WILLIE: [*Violently.*] Yes!

WINNIE: [*Same voice.*] Fear no more the heat o' the sun.
    [*Pause.*] Did you hear that?

WILLIE: [*Irritated.*] Yes.

WINNIE: [*Same voice.*] What? [*Pause.*] What?

WILLIE: [*More irritated.*] Fear no more.
    [*Pause.*]

WINNIE: [*Same voice.*] No more what? [*Pause.*] Fear no more what?

WILLIE: [*Violently.*] Fear no more!

WINNIE: [*Normal voice, gabbled.*] Bless you Willie I do
    appreciate your goodness I know what an effort it costs
    you, now you may relax I shall not trouble you again
    unless I am obliged to, by that I mean unless I come to
    the end of my own resources which is most unlikely, just

15

to know that in theory you can hear me even though in fact you don't is all I need, just to feel you there within earshot and conceivably on the qui vive is all I ask, not to say anything I would not wish you to hear or liable to cause you pain, not to be just babbling away on trust as it is were not knowing and something gnawing at me. [*Pause for breath.*] Doubt. [*Places index and second finger on heart area, moves them about, brings them to rest.*] Here. [*Moves them slightly.*] Abouts. [*Hand away.*] Oh no doubt the time will come when before I can utter a word I must make sure you heard the one that went before and then no doubt another come another time when I must learn to talk to myself a thing I could never bear to do such wilderness. [*Pause.*] Or gaze before me with compressed lips. [*She does so.*] All day long. [*Gaze and lips again.*] No. [*Smile.*] No no. [*Smile off.*] There is of course the bag. [*Turns towards it.*] There will always be the bag. [*Back front.*] Yes, I suppose so. [*Pause.*] Even when you are gone, Willie. [*She turns a little towards him.*] You *are* going, Willie, aren't you? [*Pause. Louder.*] You *will* be going soon, Willie, won't you? [*Pause. Louder.*] Willie! [*Pause. She cranes back and down to look at him.*] So you have taken off your straw, that is wise. [*Pause.*] You do look snug, I must say, with your chin on your hands and the old blue eyes like saucers in the shadows. [*Pause.*] Can you see me from there I wonder, I still wonder. [*Pause.*] No? [*Back front.*] Oh I know it does not follow when two are gathered together – [*faltering*] – in this way – [*normal*] – that because one sees the other the other sees the one, life has taught me that . . . too. [*Pause.*] Yes, life I suppose, there is no other word. [*She turns a little towards him.*] Could you see me, Willie, do you think, from where you are, if you were to raise your eyes in my direction? [*Turns a little further.*] Lift up your eyes to me, Willie, and tell me can you see me, do that for me, I'll lean back as far as I can. [*Does so. Pause.*] No? [*Pause.*] Well never mind. [*Turns back painfully front.*] The earth is very tight today, can it be I have put on flesh, I trust not. [*Pause. Absently, eyes lowered.*] The great heat possibly. [*Starts to pat and stroke ground.*] All things expanding, some more than others. [*Pause. Patting and stroking.*] Some less. [*Pause. Do.*] Oh I can well imagine what is passing through your mind, it is not enough to have to listen to the woman, now I must look at her as well. [*Pause. Do.*] Well it is very understandable. [*Pause. Do.*] Most understandable. [*Pause. Do.*] One does not appear to be asking a great deal, indeed at times it would seem hardly possible – [*voice breaks, falls to a murmur*] – to ask less – of a fellow-creature – to put it mildly – whereas actually – when you think about it – look into your heart – see the other – what he needs – peace – to be left in peace – then perhaps the moon – all this time – asking for the moon. [*Pause. Stroking hand suddenly still. Lively.*] Oh I say, what have we here? [*Bending head to ground, incredulous.*] Looks like life of some kind! [*Looks for spectacles, puts them on, bends closer. Pause.*] An emmet! [*Recoils. Shrill.*] Willie, an emmet, a live emmet! [*Seizes magnifying-glass, bends to ground again, inspects through glass.*] Where's it gone? [*Inspects.*] Ah! [*Follows its progress through grass.*] Has like a little white ball in its arms. [*Follows progress. Hand still. Pause.*] It's gone in. [*Continues a moment to gaze at spot through glass, then slowly straightens up, lays down glass, takes off spectacles and gazes before her, spectacles in hand. Finally.*] Like a little white ball. [*Long pause. Gesture to lay down spectacles.*]

WILLIE: Eggs.

WINNIE: [*Arresting gesture.*] What?

[*Pause.*]

WILLIE: Eggs. [*Pause. Gesture to lay down glasses.*] Formication.

WINNIE: [*Arresting gesture.*] What?

[*Pause.*]

WILLIE: Formication.

[*Pause. She lays down spectacles, gazes before her. Finally.*]

WINNIE: [*Murmur.*] God. [*Pause.* WILLIE *laughs quietly. After a moment she joins in. They laugh quietly together.* WILLIE *stops. She laughs on a moment alone.* WILLIE *joins in. They laugh together. She stops.* WILLIE *laughs on a moment alone. He stops. Pause. Normal voice.*] Ah well what a joy in any case to hear you laugh again, Willie, I was convinced I never would, you never would. [*Pause.*] I suppose some people might think us a trifle irreverent, but I doubt it. [*Pause.*] How can one better magnify the Almighty than by sniggering with him at his little jokes, particularly the poorer ones? [*Pause.*] I think you would back me up there, Willie. [*Pause.*] Or were we perhaps diverted by two quite different things? [*Pause.*] Oh well, what does it matter, that is what I always say, so long as one . . . you know . . . what is that wonderful line . . . laughing wild . . . something something laughing wild amid severest woe. [*Pause.*] And now? [*Long pause.*] Was I lovable once, Willie? [*Pause.*] Was I ever lovable? [*Pause.*] Do not misunderstand my question, I am not asking you if you loved me, we know all about that, I am asking you if you found me lovable – at one stage. [*Pause.*] No? [*Pause.*] You can't? [*Pause.*] Well I admit it is a teaser. And you have done more than your bit already, for the time being, just lie back now and relax, I shall not trouble you again unless I am compelled to, just to know you are there within hearing and conceivably on the semi-alert is . . . er . . . paradise enow. [*Pause.*] The day is now well advanced. [*Smile.*] To speak in the old style. [*Smile off.*] And yet it is perhaps a little soon for my song. [*Pause.*] To sing too soon is a great mistake, I find. [*Turning towards bag.*] There is of course the bag. [*Looking at bag.*] The bag. [*Back front.*] Could I enumerate its contents? [*Pause.*] No. [*Pause.*] Could I, if some kind person were to come along and ask, What all have you got in that big

black bag, Winnie? give an exhaustive answer? [*Pause.*] No. [*Pause.*] The depths in particular, who knows what treasures. [*Pause.*] What comforts. [*Turns to look at bag.*] Yes, there is the bag. [*Back front.*] But something tells me, Do not overdo the bag, Winnie, make use of it of course, let it help you . . . along, when stuck, by all means, but cast your mind forward, something tells me, cast your mind forward, Winnie, to the time when words must fail – [*she closes eyes, pause, opens eyes*] – and do not overdo the bag. [*Pause. She turns to look at bag.*] Perhaps just one quick dip. [*She turns back front, closes eyes, throws out left arm, plunges hand in bag and brings out revolver. Disgusted.*] You again! [*She opens eyes, brings revolver front and contemplates it. She weighs it in her palm.*] You'd think the weight of this thing would bring it down among the . . . last rounds. But no. It doesn't. Ever uppermost, like Browning. [*Pause.*] Brownie . . . [*Turning a little towards* WILLIE.] Remember Brownie, Willie? [*Pause.*] Remember how you used to keep on at me to take it away from you? Take it away, Winnie, take it away, before I put myself out of my misery. [*Back front. Derisive.*] *Your* misery! [*To revolver.*] Oh I suppose it's a comfort to know you're there, but I'm tired of you. [*Pause.*] I'll leave you out, that's what I'll do. [*She lays revolver on ground to her right.*] There, that's your home from this day out. [*Smile.*] The old style! [*Smile off.*] And now? [*Long pause.*] Is gravity what it was, Willie, I fancy not. [*Pause.*] Yes, the feeling more and more that if I were not held – [*gesture*] – in this way, I would simply float up into the blue. [*Pause.*] And that perhaps some day the earth will yield and let me go, the pull is so great, yes, crack all round me and let me out. [*Pause.*] Don't you ever have that feeling, Willie, of being sucked up? [*Pause.*] Don't you have to cling on sometimes, Willie? [*Pause. She turns a little towards him.*] Willie.
[*Pause.*]

WILLIE: *Sucked* up?

WINNIE: Yes love, up into the blue, like gossamer. [*Pause.*]
No? [*Pause.*] You don't? [*Pause.*] Ah well, natural laws,
natural laws, I suppose it's like everything else, it all
depends on the creature you happen to be. All I can say
for my part is that for me they are not what they were
when I was young and . . . foolish and . . . [*faltering, head
down*] . . . beautiful . . . possibly . . . lovely . . . in a way
. . . to look at. [*Pause. Head up.*] Forgive me, Willie,
sorrow keeps breaking in. [*Normal voice.*] Ah well what a
joy in any case to know you are there, as usual, and
perhaps awake, and perhaps taking all this in, some of all
this, what a happy day for me . . . it will have been.
[*Pause.*] So far. [*Pause.*] What a blessing nothing grows,
imagine if all this stuff were to start growing. [*Pause.*]
Imagine. [*Pause.*] Ah yes, great mercies. [*Long pause.*] I
can say no more. [*Pause.*] For the moment. [*Pause. Turns
to look at bag. Back front. Smile.*] No no. [*Smile off. Looks
at parasol.*] I suppose I might – [*takes up parasol*] – yes, I
suppose I might . . . hoist this thing now. [*Begins to unfurl
it. Following punctuated by mechanical difficulties overcome.*]
One keeps putting off – putting up – for fear of putting
up – too soon – and the day goes by – quite by – without
one's having put up – at all. [*Parasol now fully open. Turned
to her right she twirls it idly this way and that.*] Ah yes, so
little to say, so little to do, and the fear so great, certain
days, of finding oneself . . . left, with hours still to run,
before the bell for sleep, and nothing more to say,
nothing more to do, that the days go by, certain days go
by, quite by, the bell goes, and little or nothing said, little
or nothing done. [*Raising parasol.*] That is the danger.
[*Turning front.*] To be guarded against. [*She gazes front,
holding up parasol with right hand. Maximum pause.*] I
used to perspire freely. [*Pause.*] Now hardly at all.
[*Pause.*] The heat is much greater. [*Pause.*] The
perspiration much less. [*Pause.*] That is what I find so

wonderful. [*Pause.*] The way man adapts himself. [*Pause.*]
To changing conditions. [*She transfers parasol to left hand.
Long pause.*] Holding up wearies the arm. [*Pause.*] Not if
one is going along. [*Pause.*] Only if one is at rest. [*Pause.*]
That is a curious observation. [*Pause.*] I hope you heard
that, Willie, I should be grieved to think you had not
heard that. [*She takes parasol in both hands. Long pause.*]
I am weary, holding it up, and I cannot put it down.
[*Pause.*] I am worse off with it up than with it down, and
I cannot put it down. [*Pause.*] Reason says, Put it down,
Winnie, it is not helping you, put the thing down and get
on with something else. [*Pause.*] I cannot. [*Pause.*] I
cannot move. [*Pause.*] No, something must happen, in
the world, take place, some change, I cannot, if I am to
move again. [*Pause.*] Willie. [*Mildly.*] Help. [*Pause.*] No?
[*Pause.*] Bid me put this thing down, Willie, I would obey
you instantly, as I have always done, honoured and
obeyed. [*Pause.*] Please, Willie. [*Mildly.*] For pity's sake.
[*Pause.*] No? [*Pause.*] You can't? [*Pause.*] Well I don't
blame you, no, it would ill become me, who cannot
move, to blame my Willie because he cannot speak.
[*Pause.*] Fortunately I am in tongue again. [*Pause.*] That
is what I find so wonderful, my two lamps, when one
goes out the other burns brighter. [*Pause.*] Oh yes, great
mercies. [*Maximum pause. The parasol goes on fire. Smoke,
flames if feasible. She sniffs, looks up, throws parasol to her
right behind mound, cranes back to watch it burning. Pause.*]
Ah earth you old extinguisher. [*Back front.*] I presume
this has occurred before, though I cannot recall it.
[*Pause.*] Can you, Willie? [*Turns a little towards him.*] Can
you recall this having occurred before? [*Pause. Cranes
back to look at him.*] Do you know what has occurred,
Willie? [*Pause.*] Have you gone off on me again? [*Pause.*]
I do not ask if you are alive to all that is going on, I
merely ask if you have not gone off on me again. [*Pause.*]
Your eyes appear to be closed, but that has no particular

21

significance we know. [*Pause.*] Raise a finger, dear, will
you please, if you are not quite senseless. [*Pause.*] Do that
for me, Willie please, just the little finger, if you are still
conscious. [*Pause. Joyous.*] Oh all five, you are a darling
today, now I may continue with an easy mind. [*Back
front.*] Yes, what ever occurred that did not occur before
and yet . . . I wonder, yes, I confess I wonder. [*Pause.*]
With the sun blazing so much fiercer down, and hourly
fiercer, is it not natural things should go on fire never
known to do so, in this way I mean, spontaneous like.
[*Pause.*] Shall I myself not melt perhaps in the end, or
burn, oh I do not mean necessarily burst into flames, no,
just little by little be charred to a black cinder, all this –
[*ample gesture of arms*] – visible flesh. [*Pause.*] On the
other hand, did I ever know a temperate time? [*Pause.*]
No. [*Pause.*] I speak of temperate times and torrid times,
they are empty words. [*Pause.*] I speak of when I was not
yet caught – in this way – and had my legs and had the
use of my legs, and could seek out a shady place, like
you, when I was tired of the sun, or a sunny place when
I was tired of the shade, like you, and they are all empty
words. [*Pause.*] It is no hotter today than yesterday, it will
be no hotter tomorrow than today, how could it, and so
on back into the far past, forward into the far future.
[*Pause.*] And should one day the earth cover my breasts,
then I shall never have seen my breasts, no one ever
seen my breasts. [*Pause.*] I hope you caught something
of that, Willie, I should be sorry to think you had caught
nothing of all that, it is not every day I rise to such
heights. [*Pause.*] Yes, something seems to have occurred,
something has seemed to occur, and nothing has
occurred, nothing at all, you are quite right, Willie.
[*Pause.*] The sunshade will be there again tomorrow,
beside me on this mound, to help me through the day.
[*Pause. She takes up mirror.*] I take up this little glass,
I shiver it on a stone – [*does so*] – I throw it away – [*does*

22

so far behind her] – it will be in the bag again tomorrow, without a scratch, to help me through the day. [*Pause.*] No, one can do nothing. [*Pause.*] That is what I find so wonderful, the way things . . . [*voice breaks, head down*] . . . things . . . so wonderful. [*Long pause, head down. Finally turns, still bowed, to bag, brings out unidentifiable odds and ends, stuffs them back, fumbles deeper, brings out finally musical-box, winds it up, turns it on, listens for a moment holding it in both hands, huddled over it, turns back front, straightens up and listens to tune, holding box to breast with both hands. It plays the Waltz Duet 'I love you so' from The Merry Widow. Gradually happy expression. She sways to the rhythm. Music stops. Pause. Brief burst of hoarse song without words – musical-box tune – from* WILLIE. *Increase of happy expression. She lays down box.*] Oh this will have been a happy day! [*She claps hands.*] Again, Willie, again! [*Claps.*] Encore, Willie, please! [*Pause. Happy expression off.*] No? You won't do that for me? [*Pause.*] Well it is very understandable, very understandable. One cannot sing just to please someone, however much one loves them, no, song must come from the heart, that is what I always say, pour out from the inmost, like a thrush. [*Pause.*] How often I have said, in evil hours, Sing now, Winnie, sing your song, there is nothing else for it, and did not [*Pause.*] Could not. [*Pause.*] No, like the thrush, or the bird of dawning, with no thought of benefit, to oneself or anyone else. [*Pause.*] And now? [*Long pause. Low.*] Strange feeling. [*Pause. Do.*] Strange feeling that someone is looking at me. I am clear, then dim, then gone, then dim again, then clear again, and so on, back and forth, in and out of someone's eye. [*Pause. Do.*] Strange? [*Pause. Do.*] No, here all is strange. [*Pause. Normal voice.*] Something says, Stop talking now, Winnie, for a minute, don't squander all your words for the day, stop talking and do something for a change, will you? [*She raises hands and holds them open before her eyes. Apostrophic.*]

Do something! [*She closes hands.*] What claws! [*She turns to bag, rummages in it, brings out finally a nailfile, turns back front and begins to file nails. Files for a time in silence, then the following punctuated by filing.*] There floats up – into my thoughts – a Mr Shower – a Mr and perhaps a Mrs Shower – no – they are holding hands – his fiancée then more likely – or just some – loved one. [*Looks closer at nails*]. Very brittle today. [*Resumes filing.*] Shower – Shower – does the name mean anything – to you, Willie – evoke any reality, I mean – for you, Willie – don't answer if you don't – feel up to it – you have done more – than your bit – already – Shower – Shower. [*Inspects filed nails.*] Bit more like it. [*Raises head, gazes front.*] Keep yourself nice, Winnie, that's what I always say, come what may, keep yourself nice. [*Pause. Resumes filing.*] Yes – Shower – Shower – [*stops filing, raises head, gazes front, pause*] – or Cooker, perhaps I should say Cooker. [*Turning a little towards* WILLIE.] Cooker, Willie, does Cooker strike a chord? [*Pause. Turns a little further. Louder.*] Cooker, Willie, does Cooker ring a bell, the name Cooker? [*Pause. She cranes back to look at him. Pause.*] Oh really! [*Pause.*] Have you no handkerchief, darling? [*Pause.*] Have you no delicacy? [*Pause.*] Oh, Willie, you're not eating it! Spit it out, dear, spit it out! [*Pause. Back front.*] Ah well, I suppose it's only natural. [*Break in voice.*] Human. [*Pause. Do.*] What *is* one to do? [*Head down. Do.*] All day long. [*Pause. Do.*] Day after day. [*Pause. Head up. Smile. Calm.*] The old style! [*Smile off. Resumes nails.*] No, done him. [*Passes on to next.*] Should have put on my glasses. [*Pause.*] Too late now. [*Finishes left hand, inspects it.*] Bit more human. [*Starts right hand. Following punctuated as before.*] Well anyway – this man Shower – or Cooker – no matter – and the woman – hand in hand – in the other hands bags – kind of big brown grips – standing there gaping at me – and at last this man Shower – or Cooker – ends in 'er anyway –

stake my life on that – What's she doing? he says – What's
the idea? he says – stuck up to her diddies in the bleeding
ground – coarse fellow – What does it mean? he says –
What's it meant to mean? – and so on – lot more stuff
like that – usual drivel – Do you hear me? he says – I do,
she says, God help me – What do you mean, he says,
God help you? [*Stops filing, raises head, gazes front.*] And
you, she says, what's the idea of you, she says, what are
you meant to mean? Is it because you're still on your two
flat feet, with your old ditty full of tinned muck and
changes of underwear, dragging me up and down this
fornicating wilderness, coarse creature, fit mate – [*with
sudden violence*] – let go of my hand and drop for God's
sake, she says, drop! [*Pause. Resumes filing.*] Why doesn't
he dig her out? he says – referring to you, my dear –
What good is she to him like that? – What good is he to
her like that? – and so on – usual tosh – Good! she says,
have a heart for God's sake – Dig her out, he says, dig
her out, no sense in her like that – Dig her out with
what? she says – I'd dig her out with my bare hands, he
says – must have been man and – wife. [*Files in silence.*]
Next thing they're away – hand in hand – and the bags –
dim – then gone – last human kind – to stray this way.
[*Finishes right hand, inspects it, lays down file, gazes front.*]
Strange thing, time like this, drift up into the mind.
[*Pause.*] Strange? [*Pause.*] No, here all is strange. [*Pause.*]
Thankful for it in any case. [*Voice breaks.*] Most thankful.
[*Head down. Pause. Head up. Calm.*] Bow and raise the
head, bow and raise, always that. [*Pause.*] And now?
[*Long pause. Starts putting things back in bag, toothbrush
last. This operation, interrupted by pauses as indicated,
punctuates following.*] It is perhaps a little soon – to make
ready – for the night – [*stops tidying, head up, smile*] – the
old style! – [*smile off, resumes tidying*] – and yet I do –
make ready for the night – feeling it at hand – the bell for
sleep – saying to myself – Winnie – it will not be long

now, Winnie – until the bell for sleep. [*Stops tidying, head up.*] Sometimes I am wrong. [*Smile.*] But not often. [*Smile off.*] Sometimes all is over, for the day, all done, all said, all ready for the night, and the day not over, far from over, the night not ready, far, far from ready. [*Smile.*] But not often. [*Smile off.*] Yes, the bell for sleep, when I feel it at hand, and so make ready for the night – [*gesture*] – in this way, sometimes I am wrong – [*smile*] – but not often. [*Smile off. Resumes tidying.*] I used to think – I say I used to think – that all these things – put back into the bag – if too soon – put back too soon – could be taken out again – if necessary – if needed – and so on – indefinitely – back into the bag – back out of the bag – until the bell – went. [*Stops tidying, head up, smile.*] But no. [*Smile broader.*] No no. [*Smile off. Resumes tidying.*] I suppose this – might seem strange – this – what shall I say – this what I have said – yes – [*she takes up revolver*] – strange – [*she turns to put revolver in bag*] – were it not – [*about to put revolver in bag she arrests gesture and turns back front*] – were it not – [*she lays down revolver to her right, stops tidying, head up*] – that all seems strange. [*Pause.*] Most strange. [*Pause.*] Never any change. [*Pause.*] And more and more strange [*Pause. She bends to mound again, takes up last object, i.e. toothbrush, and turns to put it in bag when her attention is drawn to disturbance from* WILLIE. *She cranes back and to her right to see. Pause.*] Weary of your hole, dear? [*Pause.*] Well I can understand that. [*Pause.*] Don't forget your straw. [*Pause.*] Not the crawler you were, poor darling. [*Pause.*] No, not the crawler I gave my heart to. [*Pause.*] The hands and knees, love, try the hands and knees. [*Pause.*] The knees! The knees! [*Pause.*] What a curse, mobility! [*She follows with eyes his progress towards her behind mound, i.e. towards place he occupied at beginning of act.*] Another foot, Willie, and you're home. [*Pause as she observes last foot.*] Ah! [*Turns back front laboriously, rubs neck.*] Crick in my neck admiring you. [*Rubs neck.*] But it's worth it, well worth it. [*Turning slightly towards him.*] Do you know what I dream sometimes? [*Pause.*] What I dream sometimes, Willie. [*Pause.*] That you'll come round and live this side where I could see you. [*Pause. Back front.*] I'd be a different woman. [*Pause.*] Unrecognizable. [*Turning slightly towards him.*] Or just now and then, come round this side just every now and then and let me feast on you. [*Back front.*] But you can't, I know. [*Head down.*] I know. [*Pause. Head up.*] Well anyway – [*looks at toothbrush in her hand*] – can't be long now – [*looks at brush*] – until the bell. [*Top back of* WILLIE*'s head appears above slope.* WINNIE *looks closer at brush.*] Fully guaranteed . . . [*head up*] . . . what's this it was? [WILLIE*'s hand appears with handkerchief, spreads it on skull, disappears.*] Genuine pure . . . fully guaranteed . . . [WILLIE*'s hand appears with boater, settles it on head, rakish angle, disappears*] . . . genuine pure . . . ah! hog's setae. [*Pause.*] What is a hog exactly? [*Pause. Turns slightly towards* WILLIE.] What exactly is a hog, Willie, do you know, I can't remember. [*Pause. Turning a little further, pleading.*] What *is* a hog, Willie, please! [*Pause.*]

WILLIE: Castrated male swine. [*Happy expression appears on* WINNIE*'s face.*] Reared for slaughter. [*Happy expression increases.* WILLIE *opens newspaper, hands invisible. Tops of yellow sheets appear on either side of his head.* WINNIE *gazes before her with happy expression.*]

WINNIE: Oh this *is* a happy day! This will have been another happy day! [*Pause.*] After all. [*Pause.*] So far.
[*Pause. Happy expression off.* WILLIE *turns page. Pause. He turns another page. Pause.*]

WILLIE: Opening for smart youth.
[*Pause.* WINNIE *takes off hat, turns to put it in bag, arrests gesture, turns back front. Smile.*]

WINNIE: No. [*Smile broader.*] No no. [*Smile off. Puts on hat again, gazes front, pause.*] And now? [*Pause.*] Sing. [*Pause.*]

27

Sing your song, Winnie. [*Pause.*] No? [*Pause.*] Then pray.
[*Pause.*] Pray your prayer, Winnie.
[*Pause.* WILLIE *turns page. Pause.*]

WILLIE: Wanted bright boy.
[*Pause.* WILLIE *gazes before her.* WILLIE *turns page. Pause.*
Newspaper disappears. Long pause.]

WINNIE: Pray your old prayer, Winnie.
[*Long pause.*]

CURTAIN

Act Two

Scene as before.

  WINNIE *embedded up to neck, hat on head, eyes closed. Her head, which she can no longer turn, nor bow, nor raise, faces front motionless throughout act. Movements of eyes as indicated.*

  Bag and parasol as before. Revolver conspicuous to her right on mound.

  Long pause.

  Bell rings loudly. She opens eyes at once. Bell stops. She gazes front. Long pause.

WINNIE: Hail, holy light. [*Long pause. She closes her eyes. Bell rings loudly. She opens eyes at once. Bell stops. She gazes front. Long smile. Smile off. Long pause.*] Someone is looking at me still. [*Pause.*] Caring for me still. [*Pause.*] That is what I find so wonderful. [*Pause.*] Eyes on my eyes. [*Pause.*] What is that unforgettable line? [*Pause. Eyes right.*] Willie. [*Pause. Louder.*] Willie. [*Pause. Eyes front.*] May one still speak of time? [*Pause.*] Say it is a long time now, Willie, since I saw you. [*Pause.*] Since I heard you [*Pause.*] May one? [*Pause.*] One does. [*Smile.*] The old style! [*Smile off.*] There is so little one can speak of. [*Pause.*] One speaks of it all. [*Pause.*] All one can. [*Pause.*] I used to think . . . [*pause*] . . . I say I used to think that I would learn to talk alone. [*Pause.*] By that I mean to myself, the wilderness. [*Smile.*] But no. [*Smile broader.*] No no. [*Smile off.*] Ergo you are there. [*Pause.*] Oh no doubt you are dead, like the others, no doubt you have died, or gone away and left me, like the others, it doesn't matter, you are there. [*Pause. Eyes left.*] The bag too is there, the same as ever, I can see it. [*Pause. Eyes right. Louder.*] The bag is there, Willie, as good as ever, the one

29

you gave me that day . . . to go to market. [*Pause. Eyes front.*] That day. [*Pause.*] What day? [*Pause.*] I used to pray. [*Pause.*] I say I used to pray. [*Pause.*] Yes, I must confess I did. [*Smile.*] Not now. [*Smile broader.*] No no. [*Smile off. Pause.*] Then . . . now . . . what difficulties here, for the mind. [*Pause.*] To have been always what I am – and so changed from what I was. [*Pause.*] I am the one, I say the one, then the other. [*Pause.*] Now the one, then the other. [*Pause.*] There is so little one can say, one says it all. [*Pause.*] All one can. [*Pause.*] And no truth in it anywhere. [*Pause.*] My arms. [*Pause.*] My breasts. [*Pause.*] What arms? [*Pause.*] What breasts? [*Pause.*] Willie. [*Pause.*] What Willie? [*Sudden vehement affirmation.*] My Willie! [*Eyes right, calling.*] Willie! [*Pause. Louder.*] Willie! [*Pause. Eyes front.*] Ah well, not to know, not to know for sure, great mercy, all I ask. [*Pause.*] Ah yes . . . then . . . now . . . beechen green . . . this . . . Charlie . . . kisses . . . this . . . all that . . . deep trouble for the mind. [*Pause.*] But it does not trouble mine. [*Smile.*] Not now. [*Smile broader.*] No no. [*Smile off. Long pause. She closes eyes. Bell rings loudly. She opens eyes. Pause.*] Eyes float up that seem to close in peace . . . to see . . . in peace. [*Pause.*] Not mine. [*Smile.*] Not now. [*Smile broader.*] No no. [*Smile off. Long pause.*] Willie. [*Pause.*] Do you think the earth has lost its atmosphere, Willie? [*Pause.*] Do you, Willie? [*Pause.*] You have no opinion? [*Pause.*] Well that is like you, you never had any opinion about anything. [*Pause.*] It's understandable. [*Pause.*] Most. [*Pause.*] The earth ball. [*Pause.*] I sometimes wonder. [*Pause.*] Perhaps not quite all. [*Pause.*] There always remains something. [*Pause.*] Of everything. [*Pause.*] Some remains. [*Pause.*] If the mind were to go. [*Pause.*] It won't of course. [*Pause.*] Not quite. [*Pause.*] Not mine. [*Smile.*] Not now. [*Smile broader.*] No no. [*Smile off. Long pause.*] It might be the eternal cold. [*Pause.*] Everlasting perishing cold. [*Pause.*] Just chance,

I take it, happy chance. [*Pause.*] Oh yes, great mercies,
great mercies. [*Pause.*] And now? [*Long pause.*] The face.
[*Pause.*] The nose. [*She squints down.*] I can see it . . .
[*squinting down*] . . . the tip . . . the nostrils . . . breath of
life . . . that curve you so admired . . . [*pouts*] . . . a hint
of lip . . . [*pouts again*] . . . if I pout them out . . . [*sticks
out tongue*] . . . the tongue of course . . . you so admired
. . . if I stick it out . . . [*sticks it out again*] . . . the tip . . .
[*eyes up*] . . . suspicion of brow . . . eyebrow . . .
imagination possibly . . . [*eyes left*] . . . cheek . . . no . . .
[*eyes right*] . . . no . . . [*distends cheeks*] . . . even if I puff
them out . . . [*eyes left, distends cheeks again*] . . . no . . . no
damask. [*Eyes front.*] That is all. [*Pause.*] The bag of
course . . . [*eyes left*] . . . a little blurred perhaps . . . but
the bag. [*Eyes front. Offhand.*] The earth of course and
sky. [*Eyes right.*] The sunshade you gave me . . . that day
. . . [*pause*] . . . that day . . . the lake . . . the reeds. [*Eyes
front. Pause.*] What day? [*Pause.*] What reeds? [*Long pause.
Eyes close. Bell rings loudly. Eyes open. Pause. Eyes right.*]
Brownie of course. [*Pause.*] You remember Brownie,
Willie, I can see him. [*Pause.*] Brownie is there, Willie,
beside me. [*Pause. Loud.*] Brownie is there, Willie. [*Pause.
Eyes front.*] That is all. [*Pause.*] What would I do without
them? [*Pause.*] What would I do without them, when
words fail? [*Pause.*] Gaze before me, with compressed
lips. [*Long pause while she does so.*] I cannot. [*Pause.*] Ah
yes, great mercies, great mercies. [*Long pause. Low.*]
Sometimes I hear sounds. [*Listening expression. Normal
voice.*] But not often. [*Pause.*] They are a boon, sounds
are a boon, they help me . . . through the day. [*Smile.*]
The old style! [*Smile off.*] Yes, those are happy days, when
there are sounds. [*Pause.*] When I hear sounds. [*Pause.*]
I used to think . . . [*pause*] . . . I say I used to think they
were in my head. [*Smile.*] But no. [*Smile broader.*] No no.
[*Smile off.*] That was just logic. [*Pause.*] Reason. [*Pause.*]
I have not lost my reason. [*Pause.*] Not yet. [*Pause.*] Not

all. [*Pause.*] Some remains. [*Pause.*] Sounds. [*Pause.*] Like
little . . . sunderings, little falls . . . apart. [*Pause. Low.*]
It's things, Willie. [*Pause. Normal voice.*] In the bag,
outside the bag. [*Pause.*] Ah yes, things have their life,
that is what I always say, *things* have a life. [*Pause.*] Take
my looking-glass, it doesn't need me. [*Pause.*] The bell.
[*Pause.*] It hurts like a knife. [*Pause.*] A gouge. [*Pause.*]
One cannot ignore it. [*Pause.*] How often . . . [*pause*] . . .
I say how often I have said, Ignore it, Winnie, ignore the
bell, pay no heed, just sleep and wake, sleep and wake, as
you please, open and close the eyes, as you please, or in
the way you find most helpful. [*Pause.*] Open and close
the eyes, Winnie, open and close, always that. [*Pause.*]
But no. [*Smile.*] Not now. [*Smile broader.*] No no. [*Smile
off. Pause.*] What now? [*Pause.*] What now, Willie? [*Long
pause.*] There is my story of course, when all else fails.
[*Pause.*] A life. [*Smile.*] A long life. [*Smile off.*] Beginning
in the womb, where life used to begin, Mildred has
memories, she will have memories, of the womb, before
she dies, the mother's womb. [*Pause.*] She is now four or
five already and has recently been given a big waxen
dolly. [*Pause.*] Fully clothed, complete outfit. [*Pause.*]
Shoes, socks, undies, complete set, frilly frock, gloves.
[*Pause.*] White mesh. [*Pause.*] A little white straw hat with
a chin elastic. [*Pause.*] Pearly necklace. [*Pause.*] A little
picture-book with legends in real print to go under her
arm when she takes her walk. [*Pause.*] China blue eyes
that open and shut. [*Pause. Narrative.*] The sun was not
well up when Milly rose, descended the steep . . . [*pause*]
. . . slipped on her nightgown, descended all alone the
steep wooden stairs, backwards on all fours, though she
had been forbidden to do so, entered the . . . [*pause*] . . .
tiptoed down the silent passage, entered the nursery and
began to undress Dolly. [*Pause.*] Crept under the table
and began to undress Dolly. [*Pause.*] Scolding her . . . the
while. [*Pause.*] Suddenly a mouse – [*Long pause.*] Gently,

Winnie. [*Long pause. Calling.*] Willie! [*Pause. Louder.*]
Willie! [*Pause. Mild reproach.*] I sometimes find your
attitude a little strange, Willie, all this time, it is not like
you to be wantonly cruel. [*Pause.*] Strange? [*Pause.*] No.
[*Smile.*] Not here. [*Smile broader.*] Not now. [*Smile off.*]
And yet . . . [*Suddenly anxious.*] I do hope nothing is
amiss. [*Eyes right, loud.*] Is all well, dear? [*Pause. Eyes
front. To herself.*] God grant he did not go in head
foremost! [*Eyes right, loud.*] You're not stuck, Willie?
[*Pause. Do.*] You're not jammed, Willie? [*Eyes front,
distressed.*] Perhaps he is crying out for help all this time
and I do not hear him! [*Pause.*] I do of course hear cries.
[*Pause.*] But they are in my head surely. [*Pause.*] Is it
possible that . . . [*Pause. With finality.*] No no, my head
was always full of cries. [*Pause.*] Faint confused cries.
[*Pause.*] They come. [*Pause.*] Then go. [*Pause.*] As on a
wind. [*Pause.*] That is what I find so wonderful. [*Pause.*]
They cease. [*Pause.*] Ah yes, great mercies, great mercies.
[*Pause.*] The day is now well advanced. [*Smile. Smile off.*]
And yet it is perhaps a little soon for my song. [*Pause.*] To
sing too soon is fatal, I always find. [*Pause.*] On the other
hand it is possible to leave it too late. [*Pause.*] The bell
goes for sleep and one has not sung. [*Pause.*] The whole
day has flown – [*smile, smile off*] – flown by, quite by, and
no song of any class, kind or description. [*Pause.*] There
is a problem here. [*Pause.*] One cannot sing . . . just like
that, no. [*Pause.*] It bubbles up, for some unknown
reason, the time is ill chosen, one chokes it back. [*Pause.*]
One says, Now is the time, it is now or never, and one
cannot. [*Pause.*] Simply cannot sing. [*Pause.*] Not a note.
[*Pause.*] Another thing, Willie, while we are on this
subject. [*Pause.*] The sadness after song. [*Pause.*] Have
you run across that, Willie? [*Pause.*] In the course of your
experience. [*Pause.*] No? [*Pause.*] Sadness after intimate
sexual intercourse one is familiar with of course. [*Pause.*]
You would concur with Aristotle there, Willie, I fancy.

33

[*Pause.*] Yes, that one knows and is prepared to face.
[*Pause.*] But after song . . . [*Pause.*] It does not last of
course. [*Pause.*] That is what I find so wonderful. [*Pause.*]
It wears away. [*Pause.*] What are those exquisite lines?
[*Pause.*] Go forget me why should something o'er that
something shadow fling . . . go forget me . . . why should
sorrow . . . brightly smile . . . go forget me . . . never
hear me . . . sweetly smile . . . brightly sing . . . [*Pause.
With a sigh.*] One loses one's classics. [*Pause.*] Oh not
all. [*Pause.*] A part. [*Pause.*] A part remains. [*Pause.*]
That is what I find so wonderful, a part remains, of one's
classics, to help one through the day. [*Pause.*] Oh yes,
many mercies, many mercies. [*Pause.*] And now? [*Pause.*]
And now, Willie? [*Long pause.*] I call to the eye of the
mind . . . Mr Shower – or Cooker. [*She closes her eyes. Bell
rings loudly. She opens her eyes. Pause.*] Hand in hand, in
the other hands bags. [*Pause.*] Getting on . . . in life.
[*Pause.*] No longer young, not yet old. [*Pause.*] Standing
there gaping at me. [*Pause.*] Can't have been a bad
bosom, he says, in its day. [*Pause.*] Seen worse shoulders,
he says, in my time. [*Pause.*] Does she feel her legs? he
says. [*Pause.*] Is there any life in her legs? he says. [*Pause.*]
Has she anything on underneath? he says. [*Pause.*] Ask
her, he says, I'm shy. [*Pause.*] Ask her what? she says.
[*Pause.*] Is there any life in her legs. [*Pause.*] Has she
anything on underneath. [*Pause.*] Ask her yourself, she
says. [*Pause. With sudden violence.*] Let go of me for Christ
sake and drop! [*Pause. Do.*] Drop dead! [*Smile.*] But no.
[*Smile broader.*] No no. [*Smile off.*] I watch them recede.
[*Pause.*] Hand in hand – and the bags. [*Pause.*] Dim.
[*Pause.*] Then gone. [*Pause.*] Last human kind – to stray
this way. [*Pause.*] Up to date. [*Pause.*] And now? [*Pause.
Low.*] Help. [*Pause. Do.*] Help, Willie. [*Pause. Do.*] No?
[*Long pause. Narrative.*] Suddenly a mouse . . . [*Pause.*]
Suddenly a mouse ran up her little thigh and Mildred,
dropping Dolly in her fright, began to scream –

[WINNIE *gives a sudden piercing scream*] – and screamed and screamed – [WINNIE *screams twice*] – screamed and screamed and screamed and screamed till all came running, in their night attire; papa, mamma, Bibby and . . . old Annie, to see what was the matter . . . [*pause*] . . . what on earth could possibly be the matter. [*Pause.*] Too late. [*Pause.*] Too late. [*Long pause. Just audible.*] Willie. [*Pause. Normal voice.*] Ah well, not long now, Winnie, can't be long now, until the bell for sleep. [*Pause.*] Then you may close your eyes, then you *must* close your eyes – and keep them closed. [*Pause.*] Why say that again? [*Pause.*] I used to think . . . [*pause*] . . . I say I used to think there was no difference between one fraction of a second and the next. [*Pause.*] I used to say . . . [*pause*] . . . I say I used to say, Winnie, you are changeless, there is never any difference between one fraction of a second and the next. [*Pause.*] Why bring that up again? [*Pause.*] There is so little one can bring up, one brings up all. [*Pause.*] All one can. [*Pause.*] My neck is hurting me. [*Pause. With sudden violence.*] My neck is hurting me! [*Pause.*] Ah that's better. [*With mild irritation.*] Everything within reason. [*Long pause.*] I can do no more. [*Pause.*] Say no more. [*Pause.*] But I must say more. [*Pause.*] Problem here. [*Pause.*] No, something must move, in the world, I can't any more. [*Pause.*] A zephyr. [*Pause.*] A breath. [*Pause.*] What are those immortal lines? [*Pause.*] It might be the eternal dark. [*Pause.*] Black night without end. [*Pause.*] Just chance, I take it, happy chance. [*Pause.*] Oh yes, abounding mercies. [*Long pause.*] And now? [*Pause.*] And now, Willie? [*Long pause.*] That day. [*Pause.*] The pink fizz. [*Pause.*] The flute glasses. [*Pause.*] The last guest gone. [*Pause.*] The last bumper with the bodies nearly touching. [*Pause.*] The look. [*Long pause.*] What day? [*Long pause.*] What look? [*Long pause.*] I hear cries. [*Pause.*] Sing. [*Pause.*] Sing your old song, Winnie.

[*Long pause. Suddenly alert expression. Eyes switch right.*
WILLIE'*s head appears to her right round corner of mound.
He is on all fours, dressed to kill – top hat, morning coat,
striped trousers, etc., white gloves in hand. Very long bushy
white Battle of Britain moustache. He halts, gazes front,
smooths moustache. He emerges completely from behind
mound, turns to his left, halts, looks up at* WINNIE. *He
advances on all fours towards centre, halts, turns head front,
gazes front, strokes moustache, straightens tie, adjusts hat,
advances a little further, halts, takes off hat and looks up at*
WINNIE. *He is now not far from centre and within her field of
vision. Unable to sustain effort of looking up he sinks head to
ground.*]

WINNIE: [*Mondaine.*] Well this is an unexpected pleasure!
[*Pause.*] Reminds me of the day you came whining for
my hand. [*Pause.*] I worship you, Winnie, be mine. [*He
looks up.*] Life a mockery without Win. [*She goes off into
a giggle.*] What a get up, you do look a sight! [*Giggles.*]
Where are the flowers? [*Pause.*] That smile today.
[WILLIE *sinks head.*] What's that on your neck, an
anthrax? [*Pause.*] Want to watch that, Willie, before it
gets a hold on you. [*Pause.*] Where were you all this time?
[*Pause.*] What were you doing all this time? [*Pause.*]
Changing? [*Pause.*] Did you not hear me screaming for
you? [*Pause.*] Did you get stuck in your hole? [*Pause. He
looks up.*] That's right, Willie, look at me. [*Pause.*] Feast
your old eyes, Willie. [*Pause.*] Does anything remain?
[*Pause.*] Any remains? [*Pause.*] No? [*Pause.*] I haven't
been able to look after it, you know. [*He sinks his head.*]
You are still recognizable, in a way. [*Pause.*] Are you
thinking of coming to live this side now . . . for a bit
maybe? [*Pause.*] No? [*Pause.*] Just a brief call? [*Pause.*]
Have you gone deaf, Willie? [*Pause.*] Dumb? [*Pause.*] Oh
I know you were never one to talk, I worship you Winnie
be mine and then nothing from that day forth only titbits
from *Reynolds' News*. [*Eyes front. Pause.*] Ah well, what

36

matter, that's what I always say, it will have been a happy
day, after all, another happy day. [*Pause.*] Not long now,
Winnie. [*Pause.*] I hear cries. [*Pause.*] Do you ever hear
cries, Willie? [*Pause.*] No? [*Eyes back on* WILLIE.] Willie.
[*Pause.*] Look at me again, Willie. [*Pause.*] Once more,
Willie. [*He looks up. Happily.*] Ah! [*Pause. Shocked.*] What
ails you, Willie, I never saw such an expression! [*Pause.*]
Put on your hat, dear, it's the sun, don't stand on
ceremony, I won't mind. [*He drops hat and gloves and
starts to crawl up mound towards her. Gleeful.*] Oh I say, this
is terrific! [*He halts, clinging to mound with one hand,
reaching up with the other.*] Come on, dear, put a bit of
jizz into it, I'll cheer you on. [*Pause.*] Is it me you're after,
Willie . . . or is it something else? [*Pause.*] Do you want
to touch my face . . . again? [*Pause.*] Is it a kiss you're
after, Willie . . . or is it something else? [*Pause.*] There
was a time when I could have given you a hand. [*Pause.*]
And then a time before that again when I did give you a
hand. [*Pause.*] You were always in dire need of a hand,
Willie. [*He slithers back to foot of mound and lies with face
to ground.*] Brrum! [*Pause. He rises to hands and knees,
raises his face towards her.*] Have another go, Willie, I'll
cheer you on. [*Pause.*] Don't look at me like that! [*Pause.
Vehement.*] Don't look at me like that! [*Pause. Low.*] Have
you gone off your head, Willie? [*Pause. Do.*] Out of your
poor old wits, Willie? [*Pause.*]

WILLIE: [*Just audible.*] Win.

[*Pause.* WINNIE's *eyes front. Happy expression appears,
grows.*]

WINNIE: Win! [*Pause.*] Oh this *is* a happy day, this will have
been another happy day! [*Pause.*] After all. [*Pause.*] So
far. [*Pause. She hums tentatively beginning of song, then
sings softly, musical-box tune.*]

> Though I say not
> What I may not
> Let you hear,

Yet the swaying
Dance is saying,
Love me dear!
Every touch of fingers
Tells me what I know,
Says for you,
It's true, it's true,
You love me so!

[*Pause. Happy expression off. She closes her eyes. Bell rings loudly. She opens her eyes. She smiles, gazing front. She turns her eyes, smiling, to* WILLIE, *still on his hands and knees looking up at her. Smile off. They look at each other. Long pause.*]

CURTAIN